Jazzy 'n' Cool

11 Fun-Filled Solos for Early Intermediate to Intermediate Pianists

Randall Hartsell

I often motivate my piano students by allowing them to choose new music that is grounded in sound pedagogical ideas yet fun to play. *Jazzy 'n' Cool* was written to fulfill this need. It includes solid teaching material that encourages regular practice, successful performances and joyful music-making.

This book is filled with exciting music that students often describe as "cool." The rhythmic boogies, jazzy melodic lines, soulful blues and lively, syncopated pieces fit comfortably under the hand and are easy to memorize.

Play several of these pieces for your students and allow them to choose their favorite ones to learn first. Both you and your students will be pleased with the results. Best wishes for success!

Table of Contents

Backstreet Blues 2
Bebop Boogie 10
Boogie Woogie Show-off 22
Hip-Hop Groove 14
Jazzy 'n' Cool 8
Mississippi Blues 6
Moody Moods 4
New Orleans Blue 20
Sly Spy 18
Sneak Attack! 12
Syncopated Commotion 16

This collection is dedicated to Allison Senger, Kyle Jackson and Brent Sesler.

Cover illustration: Dana D'Elia

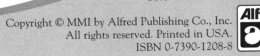

Backstreet Blues

Randall Hartsell

Moody Moods

Randall Hartsell

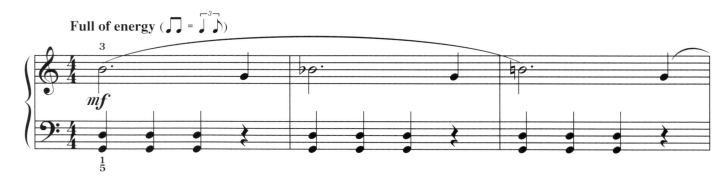

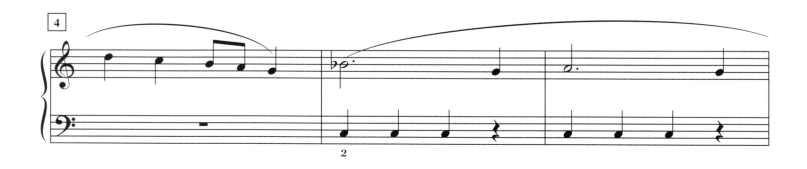

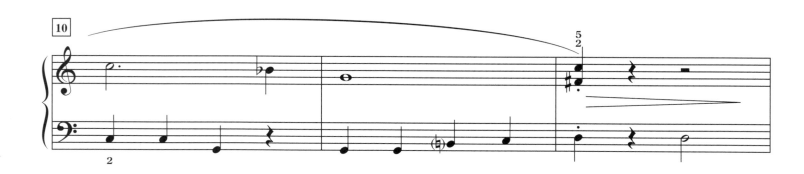

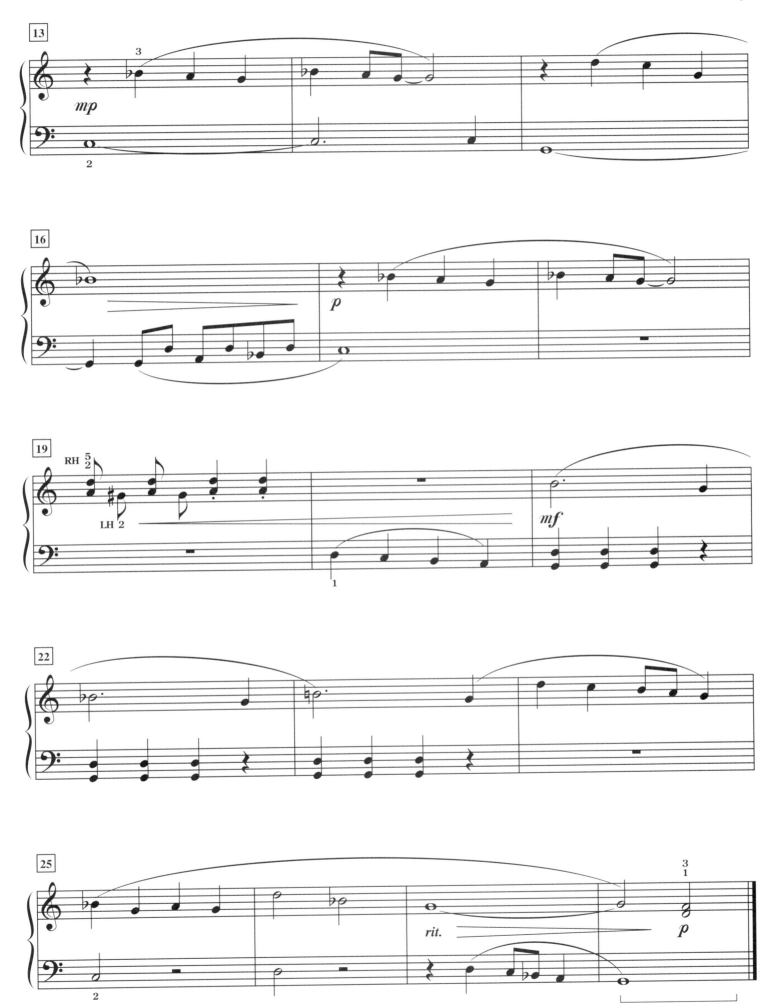

Mississippi Blues

Randall Hartsell

Jazzy 'n' Cool

Randall Hartsell

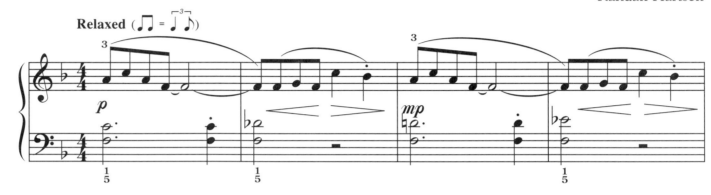

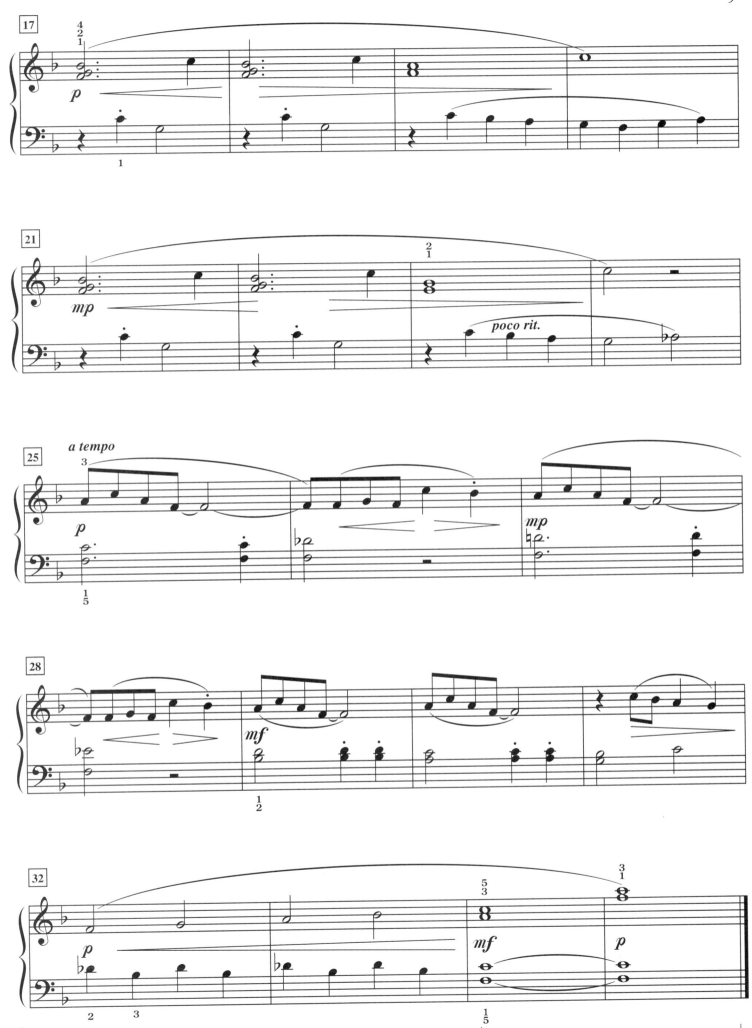

Bebop Boogie

Randall Hartsell

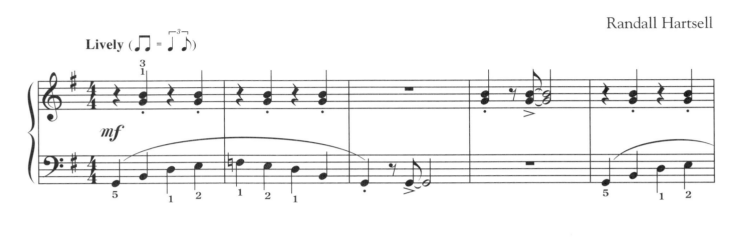

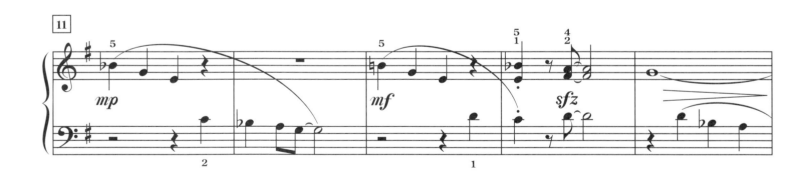

Sneak Attack!

Randall Hartsell

Hip-Hop Groove

Randall Hartsell

Syncopated Commotion

Randall Hartsell

Sly Spy

Randall Hartsell

New Orleans Blue

Randall Hartsell

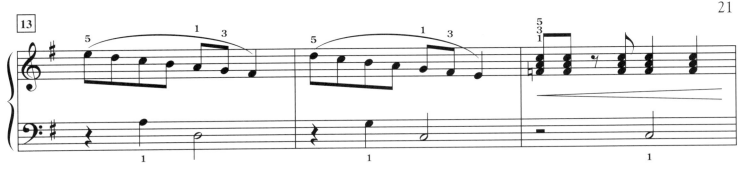

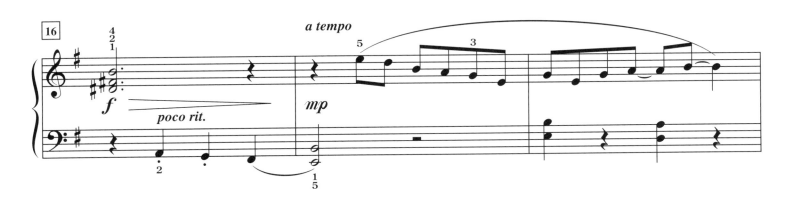

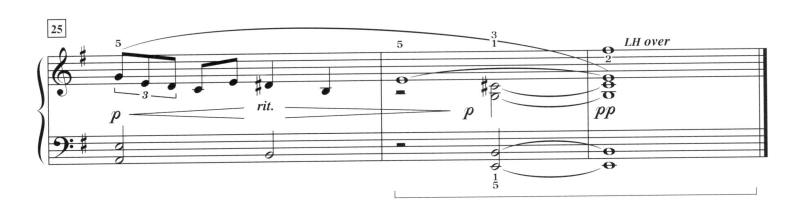

Boogie Woogie Show-off

Randall Hartsell

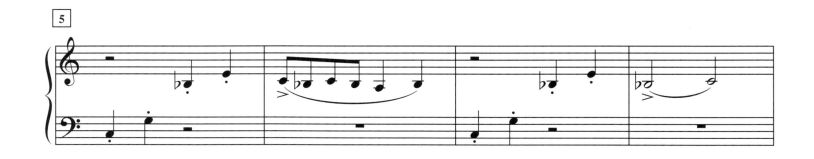

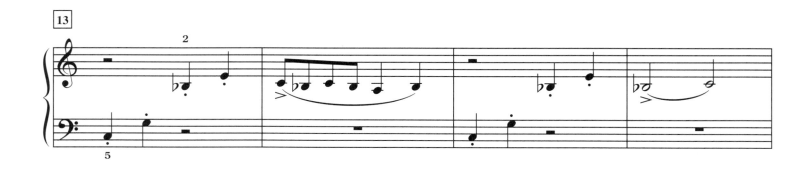

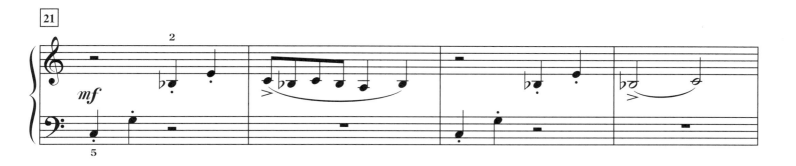

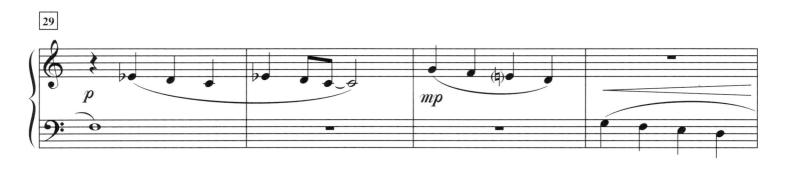